SPOOKED!

EARTH'S STRANGEST PLACES

INVESTIGATING HISTORY'S MYSTERIES

Louise Spilsbury

CHERITON
CHILDREN'S BOOKS

Published in 2024 by **Cheriton Children's Books**
1 Bank Drive West, Shrewsbury, Shropshire, SY3 9DJ, UK

© 2024 Cheriton Children's Books

First Edition

Author: Louise Spilsbury
Designer: Jessica Moon
Editor: Jennifer Sanderson
Proofreader: Ella Hammond

Picture credits: Cover: Shutterstock/Amir Bajric (fg), Shutterstock/Wangkun Jia (bg).
Inside: p1: Shutterstock/Charles Bowman, p4: Wikimedia Commons/Tormod Sandtorv,
p4t: Shutterstock/IgorZh, p5r: Shutterstock/Fotokvadrat, p5t: Shutterstock/Mike
Trachtenberg, p7b: Shutterstock/Independent Birds, p7c: Shutterstock/SusaImages, p7t:
Shutterstock/Alex Marakhovets, p8: Shutterstock/Senron, p9: Shutterstock/Subphoto.
com, p11b: Shutterstock/Stephen Bateman, p11t: Shutterstock/Richard Whitcombe,
p12: Shutterstock/Rudi Leys, p13: Shutterstock/Miki Pavlovikj, p14: Shutterstock/Natali
Glado, p15: Shutterstock/Thongchai S, p16: Shutterstock/Mirigrina, p17: Shutterstock/
jritucci, p18: Shutterstock/Space Wind, p19b: Shutterstock/Ariadne's Art, p19t:
Shutterstock/Halie Graham, p20: Shutterstock/Sergey Uryadnikov, p21tl: Shutterstock/
Arda Savasciogullari, p21tr: Shutterstock/MS7503, p22: Shutterstock/Lee Risar, p25b:
AdobeStock/Mathieu, p25t: Shutterstock/Bernard Barroso, p26: Wikimedia Commons/
Alexander Van Driessche, p27: Wikimedia Commons/Peter Andersen, p28: Shutterstock/
Netfalls Remy Musser, p29: Shutterstock/Tatiana Popova, p30: Shutterstock/ON-
Photography Germany, p31: Shutterstock/Iobard, p33b: Shutterstock/Amir Bajric, p33t:
Shutterstock/Wangkun Jia, p34: Shutterstock/Charles Bowman, p35: Shutterstock/
Rainer Fuhrmann, p36: Shutterstock/Margaret Zommers, p37: Shutterstock/Aleksandra
Wilert, p38: Shutterstock/Tero Hakala, p41b: Shutterstock/Makasana Photo, p41t:
Shutterstock/Maximillian Cabinet, p42: Shutterstock/Faraxshutter, p43c: Shutterstock/
Oleksandr Grechin, p43t: Shutterstock/Doug Meek, p45b: Shutterstock/BlackMac, p45t:
Shutterstock/Alastair Munro.

Printed in China

Please visit our website,
www.cheritonchildrensbooks.com
to see more of our high-quality books.

CONTENTS

CHAPTER 1

OUR STRANGE PLANET

Standing on solid land, our planet seems like a safe and stable place, doesn't it? But, that's not always the case. Earth is home to some weird, creepy, and downright deadly spots. These are spooky locations that you visit or enter at your **peril**. Among the most hair-raising are the strange craters, or bowl-shaped dents, that appear in the ground and threaten to swallow us up!

The Gateway to Hell

In the middle of the **barren**, quiet desert of northern Turkmenistan in Asia, a **sinister** roaring disturbs the air. The roaring comes from a gaping, fiery crater filled with flames that has been blasting out heat non-stop for years. This is the Darvaza Gas Crater, more often called the Gateway to Hell.

Accident or Evil?

The official explanation for this crater is that in 1971, geologists (scientists who study rocks) drilling for oil hit a cavern filled with natural gas. Their drilling equipment fell into the pit and the land collapsed beneath it. The air filled with dangerous fumes, which the geologists tried to burn off by setting the gas on fire. They thought the blaze would last a few weeks but the pit has been burning furiously ever since. Not everyone believes this version of events. Some people think something a lot more spooky caused the Darvaza Gas Crater. Some locals wonder if it really is an entrance to Hell.

If anything or anyone gets too close to the Darvaza Gas Crater, they will be burned to cinders in an instant.

The powerful waves and slippery rocks at Thor's Well can cause people to fall into this dangerous hole.

Thor's Well

Legend has it that long ago, Thor, the **Scandinavian** God of Thunder and Lightning, was so angry that, in a fit of rage, he struck Earth with his hammer. The impact created a dangerous, bottomless pit that swallows up water from the Pacific Ocean but, mysteriously, never fills up. The pit is known as Thor's Well and lies on the coast of Oregon.

Where Does the Water Go?

One theory is that Thor's Well is the **remains** of a large sea cave, carved out by powerful waves over many years, whose ceiling collapsed. Rough seas sometimes cause the water that disappears into the pit to shoot out in huge, explosive sprays, reaching up to 20 feet (6 m) high. Others say that the missing water runs into cavernous tunnels beneath the surface, which release it into the ocean elsewhere.

SET TO SPOOK!

In this book, we are going to explore some of the creepy reports of strange fiery pits and cursed stones, deadly swirling seas, and mysterious holes in the ground that open suddenly and devour anything above them. Some of the stories will send shivers down your spine. Some of them will leave you truly spooked!

Strange Sinkholes

Sinkholes are strange pits that can open up in the ground without any warning. Some are fairly shallow but others can reach more than 2,000 feet (610 m) deep into the earth. These monster holes have swallowed up people, cars, trees, and entire city blocks.

How Sinkholes Form

Sinkholes often happen in places where the rock below the ground is limestone or another rock that can be naturally **dissolved** and eroded, or worn away, by underground streams or rainwater. As this soft rock dissolves, caves develop beneath the surface. As the cave gets bigger, the land above it has no support, so it collapses into a sinkhole. Sometimes, people cause sinkholes by drilling or digging. They may also appear in cities if pipes below ground spring a leak.

Deadly Holes

In 2010, a gaping sinkhole suddenly tore open in Guatemala, Central America. It swallowed an entire three-story building in an instant. The sinkhole was most likely caused by rains from a heavy storm and by leaking water from an underground sewerage pipe. The water had eroded the ground underneath the city.

The Devil's Sinkhole

The Devil's Sinkhole is a terrifying black hole in Edwards County, Texas. The sinkhole is about 50 feet (15 m) wide and drops 140 feet (43 m) down into a gloomy and inky cavern. If someone fell into the hole, they would not be alone. Inside the underground cave there are huge numbers of Mexican free-tailed bats flapping about or resting. The cavity they live in was named the Devil's Sinkhole because it was said to resemble an outlet to Hell, and the name stuck. No one is allowed to enter the cavern, and few would want to!

SPOOKED!

Native Americans considered sinkholes to be sacred, or holy, because they believed they were routes to the **underworld** and the gods. Evidence such as arrowheads and other treasures from the site suggests that they used the Devil's Sinkhole to bury their dead.

Some 3 million bats emerge in a swirling mass from the Devil's Sinkhole in search of food on warm nights.

Spooky Cenotes

In Central America, sinkholes filled with water are called cenotes. Cenotes were important to the ancient Maya. They used them for water and the cenotes were also places of worship. The Maya believed these life-giving water-filled holes were also entrances to the underworld. Offerings to their gods and **ancestors** were often thrown into the pools. They also used sacred cenotes for making **sacrifices** to the gods, in particular to their rain god Chaac. Human sacrifices were made to thank the gods for the gift of water and sometimes, to request it.

A Plague?

A cenote in southern Mexico is avoided because the villagers living near it fear this underwater cave might be haunted. And, no wonder! **Archeologists** exploring the cenote found its floors littered with the remains of 15 bodies. The area was part of the Mayan Empire hundreds of years ago. A nearby Mayan city had been built around 40 sinkholes used for water. This cenote was outside the city walls. There were no signs that the bodies had been injured, so archeologists think the bones belonged to victims of a plague. A plague is a disease that infects people and spreads quickly.

Some cenotes were used only for collecting water. Others were sacred and used for worship that included human sacrifices.

Exploring the cenotes must be a strangely spooky experience.

The Sacred Cenote

There are reports of people being thrown alive as sacrifices to the gods into the Sacred Cenote in the Mayan city of Chichén Itzá. Divers venturing into this cenote found pottery and precious goods such as **jade** and gold. They also found the remains of animals and more than 200 humans. The human skulls and bones belonged to babies, children, teenagers, and adults. Around half were children, most aged between four and six. The remains showed that the victims suffered painful injuries before they were cast into these spine-chilling waters.

SPOOKED!

Before explorers dive into a cenote, local people might perform a special ceremony and cook offerings of food on a fire. The ceremony is done to ask the gods for permission to enter the cenote. It is also thought to make peace with the creature that locals believe guards a cenote: a huge feathered serpent with a horse's head. Locals fear this beast will drag children who get too close into the water.

THE GREAT BLUE

Spooky Sinkhole

Legends have always haunted the Great Blue Hole, the largest underwater sinkhole in the world. There are tales of deep-sea monsters living in the darkness in its depths. The Great Blue Hole lies off the coast of Belize in Central America. It's a perfect circle and colored a deep, rich blue. It measures an incredible 1,000 feet (305 m) across and it is more than 400 feet (122 m) deep.

How It Formed

The Great Blue Hole formed many, many years ago as a large limestone cave above the ground on dry land. Thousands of years ago, at the end of the last **Ice Age**, temperatures on Earth warmed up. The ice melted and sea levels rose. The rising tides flooded the cave, and the Great Blue Hole filled with water.

Deathly Hole

Divers and snorkelers have swum in the surface waters of the cave for many years, but few have dared to venture deeper to find what lies beyond the darkness. In 2018, a group of brave explorers in two submarines went down deep to discover the secrets at the bottom of this hole. What they found there shocked them—the bodies of two lost divers, who had gone missing in the ocean. There was also a graveyard of animals, crabs, conches, and other creatures that had fallen into the hole, sunk to the bottom, and then run out of oxygen and died.

Creatures of the Deep

The Great Blue Hole is home to several species of shark, including bull sharks, Caribbean reef sharks, and the hammerhead shark. But the animal that some people fear most is the sea monster rumored to live there. Large and deep sinkholes across the ocean have underwater caves that branch off horizontally from the main hole. People believe these deep-sea creatures lurk there.

The Great Blue Hole Monster

In 1972, a Belizean newspaper reported a sighting of the Great Blue Hole monster. Four divers all said they saw an unusual sea creature with bright blue skin and a snake-like head with large red eyes that looked like flashlights. It was the longest sea creature they had ever seen.

No one really knows if there is a monster in the Great Blue Hole but some people think that the sharks that swim there are pretty scary!

Can you imagine diving
into the darkness of the
Great Blue Hole?

CHAPTER 2

REMARKABLE ROCKS

Rocks were important to early people as they were the first tools they used. People used rocks for building homes and to help them make weapons, which they used to hunt animals for food and to protect themselves. Rocks were even rubbed together quickly to create sparks for making fire. Rocks were so important that people also used them in many of their stories. The strangest rock forms had the spookiest legends.

Lands of the Giants?

On the coast of Northern Ireland in the United Kingdom (UK) there is a dramatic rock formation made up of 40,000 huge black columns that stick out of the sea. The formation is known as the Giant's Causeway. Legends say a giant living in Northern Ireland named Finn was having trouble with another giant, Benandonner, who lived across the Irish Sea in Scotland. When Benandonner threatened Ireland, Finn was furious. He ripped rocks from the coast and hurled them into the water to make a path so he could walk over the sea to Scotland.

It's a Bad Idea!

Walking across the columns turned out to be a bad idea. Benandonner was much bigger than Finn, so Finn raced back across the walkway. Benandonner followed. Back in Ireland, Finn's quick-thinking wife disguised him as a baby. When Benandonner saw this huge "baby," he decided that if Finn's baby was that big, Finn must be enormous! So, Benandonner rushed back to Scotland, tearing up as much of the Causeway as he could, to stop Finn chasing him.

The scientific explanation for the Giant's Causeway is that 60 million years ago, lava flowed from a volcano and cooled to formed the incredible interlocking columns of rock.

SPOOKED!

High up on the peaks of Dartmoor in southern England, UK there is a giant column of rock called the Bowerman's Nose. Legend has it that local witches disliked a large, powerful hunter named Bowerman because he wasn't afraid of them and he encouraged others not to be afraid too. So, one day, they trapped Bowerman and cast a spell on him. They turned the hunter and his pack of large, fierce dogs into a column of stone. That column, with his nose sticking out, has been there ever since.

Goblin Valley

Did you know that there are goblins lurking in a remote corner of Utah? Don't worry, these are not the evil, grotesque, creatures of legends that bring trouble to humans. Instead, these are the thousands of strange and eerie rock formations found in Goblin Valley State Park. Many of the shapes resemble goblins, and that is how the valley got its name.

A Gathering of Goblins

The rock formations are called hoodoos. Hoodoos are pillars formed by layers of different kinds of rock. The layers of harder rock don't erode in the wind and rain as quickly as the layers of softer rock. This means that over time, the rock pillars erode into weird and interesting shapes. In some places, the hoodoos are close together and it looks as if the goblins are gathering in a group!

Imagine how spooky it would be to walk here at night, with the sounds of nocturnal animals haunting the darkness!

SPOOKED!

In the legends of the Native American people who once lived in Utah, the strange goblin pillars were said to be the remains of ancient beings who had been turned to stone long ago.

Rainbow Mountains

The Rainbow Mountains of China are a wonder of the world. These famous mountains are known for their incredible otherworldly colors. It looks almost as if a rainbow has been turned to stone! According to one legend, a Chinese goddess named Nüwa made them. Nüwa had created humans out of the muddy clay on the riverbank. To protect her creation from being attacked by wild, dangerous animals, Nüwa built a barrier to keep them out. She melted five different colored rocks together, forming the rainbow mountains.

Layers Through Time

Geologists have their own ideas about the mountains. They claim that they were formed over millions of years. Layers of tiny pieces of different colored rocks were pressed together over time. The rocks in higher layers were heavy, so pressed down and compacted, or squashed together, the lower layers. Then the layers buckled up into a wavy pattern as the tectonic plates that form the outer crust of Earth moved. Over thousands of years, rain and wind wearing away the rock carved the valleys and shaped the mountains.

The Rainbow Mountains must have mystified the people of ancient China!

DEATH VALLEY

Hot and Dry

Death Valley in California is one of the hottest and driest places on Earth. The fierce summer temperatures in this vast desert have caused much human suffering. According to the legends of the Native American Timbisha Shoshone people, Death Valley was once a lush, green landscape of rolling meadows, full of flowers, cascading springs, and a large lake. But, this all changed when a spoiled queen turned evil in her quest for a vast, lavish palace made from slabs of stone.

Queen of Death Valley

The Timbisha queen forced her people and even some members of her own family to work on the new palace. She punished them cruelly for not working hard enough, lashing their backs if they slowed down during the midday heat. One day, the queen even beat her own daughter. The furious princess dropped the stone she was carrying and slowly turned to look at her mother. The girl's last words were a curse against her mother the queen, and her kingdom. Then, exhausted and overcome by the heat, the princess dropped to the ground and died.

The Curse of Death Valley

The curse soon began to take effect. The Sun became hotter and this caused the plants to **wilt** and die. Lakes and streams dried up and the wild animals died or ran away. The lush, green valley turned into an empty, dry desert. Many of the queen's people died of starvation. The rest left the valley. Some legends say that points of whitened rock in the valley that look like figures are the ghosts of these ancient people. In her misery, the queen became sick and with no one left to care for her, she died alone in her unfinished palace.

Naming the Valley

The blistering daytime heat in Death Valley can kill unprepared visitors. During the Gold Rush (1848–1855) many people came to the United States to find their fortune. As they traveled across the country to reach California to mine for gold, many accidentally found themselves in the valley. In one wagon train, 13 people died in 1849. One of those who escaped the desert alive apparently said: "Goodbye, Death Valley," and the name stuck!

Did a curse turn Death Valley from a green and lush place to a barren desert?

CHAPTER 3

WEIRD WATERS

The **freshwater** streams, rivers, and lakes in our world are a source of life. Plants grow in and around them, people drink their water, and play on their banks. Yet these clear, blue waterways are quite different from the weirdest waters in our world. They include lakes and rivers that bring death, not life. Some turn animals into stone or could boil you to death. Others are even said to be home to spooky spirits that guard them. Some are just plain strange!

Hot Springs

The rocky outer layer of Earth is thinner in some places than others. That's because beneath Earth's crust, the liquid rock called magma inside the planet is hotter than the surrounding rock. This magma creates hot springs, a place where waters are weirdly hot. Some hot springs have waters that are not too hot to swim in. Others are hot enough to kill animals that enter them. At times, fierce, boiling waters within a hot spring can explode and shoot water into the air.

The Grand Prismatic Spring

The Grand Prismatic Spring is the biggest hot spring in the United States. Its incredible colors and the steam that swirls above it look like they belong to another world. In the center of the spring, it is too hot for any living things to survive. Only **microorganisms** called thermophiles, which means "heat loving," can live in the slightly less hot waters around its edge. These colorful microorganisms are what give the Grand Prismatic Spring its amazing color displays.

Fatal Waters

Although the spring is roped off for safety, more than 20 people have ignored the warnings and died from falling into the waters. The water can reach 188 degrees Fahrenheit (87° C). It can kill people in just minutes. Within just a few hours in this hot spring, an entire human body would completely dissolve into nothing.

The magma that lies beneath the surface of Yellowstone National Park heats the Grand Prismatic Spring.

SPOOKED!

The Native American people that lived in the area long ago, used the hot springs of the Yellowstone National Park for religious purposes. They believed the springs were filled with friendly and helpful spirits. They used the springs for cooking food, and bathed in the cooler water for healing. Sometimes, they buried their dead in the bubbling water.

A Lake That Turns Living Things to Stone

In ancient Greek mythology, Medusa is a monstrous creature that can turn people to stone. A lake in Tanzania in Africa is said to do the same! Lake Natron seems a peaceful and serene place but something mysterious and spine-chilling is going on in the waters. Visitors here soon realize that the dead animals surrounding the water look as if they have been petrified, or turned to stone. What are the deadly secrets of Lake Natron?

Lake Natron's Secrets

The water in Lake Natron is extremely **alkaline** because of the sodium carbonate and other minerals that flow into it from the surrounding hills. This means the water can burn the skin and eyes of animals that are not used to it. Flamingos and some of the other animals that live around the lake can cope with its stinging, burning water. But when an animal is unlucky enough to die in the lake, the sodium carbonate preserves the animal's body, making it look like a hardened shell or stone.

SPOOKED!

Lake Natron's deadly water means flamingos there can lay eggs in their nests more safely as **predators** dare not go there.

Deadly secrets lurk in Lake Natron's waters...

What happens to the disappearing water at the Devil's Kettle Waterfall?

The Devil's Kettle Waterfall

Its name tells you there must be something spooky about the Devil's Kettle Waterfall in Minnesota. At the top of the waterfall, the river splits in two. One side of the river plunges over the top and tumbles down the rocks into a pool of water at the bottom, like most waterfalls do. The other side, however, drops into a deep pit known as the Devil's Kettle. Then, the water disappears!

A Strange Vanishing Act

The secret of the Devil's Kettle Waterfall has confused people for many years. Some people have even thrown objects into the waterfall in the hope of finding them **downstream**. This would help them prove that the water in the Devil's Kettle goes under and then rejoins the river. But those objects disappeared too.

A Mystery Solved?

Scientists discovered that the water flow at the top and bottom of the Devil's Kettle were about the same. They think water disappears into the hole and then rejoins the river from underground. The scientists explain the lost objects thrown into the falls by saying they must simply be pulverized, or crushed, by the water and rocks before they can reappear downstream.

The Pink Lake

On maps all over the world, rivers and lakes are marked as blue. But it turns out this isn't always the correct choice of color... In Western Australia, when viewed from above, Lake Hillier is bright, bubblegum pink! Its water is even pink when poured into a glass. The strange water of the lake causes no harm to human skin if people swim in or touch it.

Secrets in the Water

Scientists do not fully understand the reason for Lake Hillier's pink color. Some scientists believe that the color comes from seaweed in the lake. When the water gets salty, high temperatures and sunlight make the seaweed release a natural coloring that turns the water pink. It is thought that microorganisms may also be the cause of the Lake's pink color. These **bacteria** live in the salty crust on the Lake's surface.

Spooky Lakes

There is something very strange and spooky about the three crater lakes at the top of the Kelimutu volcano in Indonesia, southeast Asia. Although these three lakes sit almost side-by-side, they are different colors and change color independently of each other, like weird volcanic mood rings! The water in the lakes can change from blood red or pitch black to gleaming turquoise and green.

SPOOKED!

Lake Hillier's pink color holds significance for local Aboriginal people. The lake is part of a **Dreamtime** creation story about a great snake that turned the water pink.

The Lakes of the Lost Souls

Locals believe the souls of their ancestors go to rest in one of the three lakes based on what they have done on Earth. One lake is said to be the resting place of people who led good lives and died in old age. The souls of those who die young end up in another lake. The third lake is the final resting place of those who have done evil things in their life.

Causes of the Colors?

Scientists think the changing colors of the lakes are caused by holes inside the volcano vents that release steam and gases. This causes mineral-rich water from the bottom of the lakes to flow to their surfaces. The different minerals and the different amounts of oxygen in the water help make the different colors.

The strange colors of its lakes and the thick mists over Kelimutu suggest to some people this is a supernatural place.

BOILING RIVER

Spooky Water

Hidden deep in the rain forest in Peru, South America, is the mysterious Boiling River. Steam rising from its bubbling turquoise waters can get as hot as 200 degrees Fahrenheit (93 °C). The water in the river is not quite boiling, but it can kill animals that fall into it. For hundreds of years, the Boiling River was thought to be just a popular legend. It was known only to local people living nearby, until a geologist found it in 2011.

Hottest River in the World

The Boiling River is impressive. Its hot water flows for 4 miles (6.4 km). In places it is up to 80 feet (24 m) wide, which is as wide as a two-lane road, and up to 15 feet (4.5 m) deep. The local name for the river is "Shanay-timpishka," which means "boiled with the heat of the Sun." The mud of the riverbank is too hot to walk on, and if you fell in, your skin would be covered in burns in less than a minute. Small, unfortunate animals such as frogs float dead in the water. Strangely, it is their eyes that seem to cook first and then turn a spooky milky-white color.

A Serpent Spirit

Few people believed the legend of the Boiling River because although hot rivers do exist, they're usually near volcanoes, and there are no volcanoes in the part of the country where the river is found. Was the river's heat caused by something spookier? Local people believed the Boiling River was home to very powerful jungle spirits. Only the most powerful **shamans** went there because other people were afraid of the spirit. At the headwaters of the Boiling River there is a boulder in the shape of a snake's head. According to legend, the spirit that lives here is a giant serpent named Yacumama, or "Mother of the Waters," that gives birth to hot and cold waters.

What Causes It?

Scientists believe they have found a different explanation for the boiling water. They say that the water is heated underground by red-hot molten rock. The water sinks down deep underground, where it is warmed by heat from the center of Earth. Then it shoots back up through cracks in the surface and flows into the river.

Perhaps a real, but unusually large, snake inspired the legend of the giant serpent named Yacumama?

CHAPTER 4

CURIOUS CAVES

The darkness, strange shadows, weird rock formations, and eerie echoes in underground caves can make you feel as if you've entered another world. As well as spectacular natural forms, some of the world's caves also hold hidden dangers and intriguing and spooky secrets.

A Healing Cave

The Giant Crystal Cave in Mexico is a unique and incredible place. Some people also think of it as a magical one. The cave lies deep underground and is filled with huge **gypsum** crystals. These sharp-edged sticks have grown over millions of years. Some people believe that gypsum crystal, also known as selenite, has healing benefits and makes people who touch it look younger.

Dangerous Depths

The problem is that getting to see the crystals is almost impossible. It is so hot in the cave that anyone who stays there for longer than 10 minutes will likely die. There is so much moisture in the air that if a person stays there for too long, the build-up of fluid in their lungs can lead to **suffocation**.

The largest crystals are up to 36 feet (11 m) long and 3.2 feet (1 m) thick, and climbing them is difficult.

The Cave of the Crystal Skeletons

Some of the creepy caves deep within the rain forest of Belize in Central America hide a dark secret. Here lie the remains of children who may have been sacrificed to please an angry god. What makes these skeletons even more spine-tingling is that their bones are covered in crystals that sparkle eerily in the lamp light. As an underground stream rich in calcium from the limestone rock in the cave washed over the bones, it formed crystals and cemented the skeletons firmly to the cave floor.

Ancient Sacrifices

The ancient Maya believed caves, such as cenotes, were one of the ways to enter the underworld. There are human skeletons in Actun Tunichil Muknal cave that are believed to be from ritual sacrifices made by the Maya to their gods more than 1,000 years ago. The skeletons range in age from one year old to adult. Almost all were killed by being hit with an object on the head. Some had their skulls crushed.

This is one of the crystal skeletons found in the Actun Tunichil Muknal cave.

SPOOKED!

There is even evidence that some Mayan victims were tied up and tortured. In one chamber in the cave, there are two stone pillars where important Mayans performed **blood rituals**, and offered up blood to the gods.

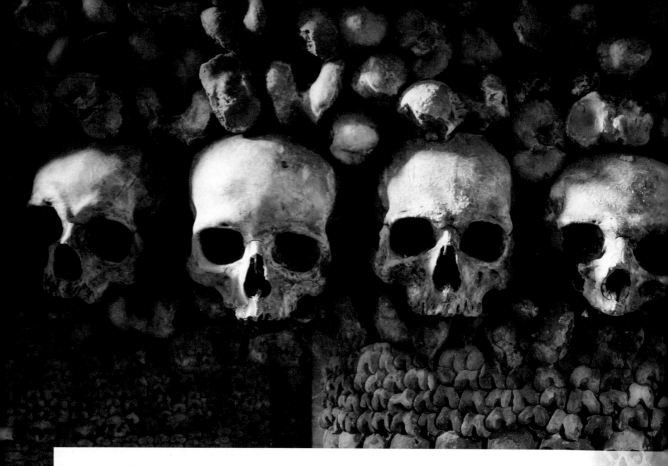

The Cave Creature

Carlsbad Caverns in New Mexico is a network of around 119 caves and the source of a mystery that has bewildered scientists for many years. The **fossilized** skeleton of a giant sloth creature was found deep below the ground in a pit beneath a chamber known as Devil's Den. The creature's bones are believed to be 11,000 years old. This means it was alive during the last Ice Age.

An Ancient Beast

Today, scientists know the bones belonged to a giant ground sloth. This ancient beast reached 9 feet (2.7 m) long and had savage claws and a big, powerful tail. Ground sloths ate plants so would have probably used their claws and tail to defend themselves from attacks by deadly predators such as giants cats and wolves. There were no plants to eat in the dark caves, however, so what was this strange creature doing there? Some geologists think that the sloth fell into Devil's Den alive and died when it got lost and couldn't find food to eat. Others think it may have been chased into the deep, dark pit by a ferocious and hungry predator.

Skull-Filled Caves

There are 6 million skeletons beneath the streets of Paris, France. These are not animal remains—they are human remains. In the 1780s, the number of people in Paris was growing and the city cemeteries were filled with many layers of graves and human remains piled on top of one another. The smell was terrible and there were so many dead bodies buried in cemeteries and beneath churches, that corpses began breaking through the walls of people's cellars. To create space, the remains of those who had been long dead were moved underground to create the Paris Catacombs.

Deathly Displays

The skull-filled caves of the Paris Catacombs are some of the eeriest underground places to visit. The Catacombs are filled with human thigh bones, skulls, and other bones. They have all been painstakingly stacked and arranged in strangely decorative, neat displays. Beside the bones are poems and quotes about death.

The Paris Catacombs hold a vast collection of bones and skulls.

SPOOKED!

A tour of the Paris Catacombs is not for the faint-hearted! Among the piles of skulls, it is possible to spot many that did not die of natural causes. For example, one skull has a perfect circle in its left cheek, suggesting the victim died from a gunshot wound to the head.

The World of the Ice Giants

In Austria, Europe, the world's biggest ice cave is a sight to behold, but for hundreds of years, most local people refused to venture into it. Local legends say that the gaping underground caves of Eisriesenwelt lead to Hell or the underworld, and whoever stepped into them would never return. Others say that the cave was home to ice giants. These were cruel and dangerous beings that could bring chaos and destruction to the world.

Icy Wonders

As a result of these terrifying tales, the cave was not explored until the nineteenth century. Today, brave visitors can see magnificent ice formations, frozen waterfalls, and an ice palace in the underground world. Nature has carved incredible ice sculptures that shimmer in blues and greens and look like shadowy giants in the distance. One cave gallery is known as Hymir's Castle, named for a legendary **Norse** ice giant. Legend has it that Hymir was a wise, yet cruel, ice giant. He had a terrible temper, so you would not want to meet him in the depths of a deep and chilly cavern!

Den of Dogs

Those visiting the Waitomo area of New Zealand step through a spectacular spiral entrance to reach the magical caves of Ruakuri. Ruakuri means "den of dogs." Local Māori people have a legend that a hunter discovered the cave. During his discovery, dogs close to the entrance attacked him. After fighting and eating the wild dogs, the hunter asked that when he died, he should be buried inside the cave. Whether or not you believe the legend, the cave was used as a Māori burial place and there are still some bodies there today.

SPOOKED!

In Māori legends, the Ruakuri caves are the entrance to the underworld. One part of this sacred cave system is known as the "ghost walk." This is the route that dead people are said to have followed to the underworld.

The legendary ice giants of Europe were terrifying and dangerous beings.

MAMMOTH CAVES

The Longest Cave

The Mammoth Cave System in Kentucky, is the longest known cave system in the world, with many of its caverns still hidden and unexplored. With more than 150 reports of creepy experiences and sightings in the caves, many of them by witnesses such as rangers and scientists, Mammoth Cave National Park is one of Earth's strangest places.

Doctor of Doom

In the 1840s, a doctor came up with the strange idea of turning the caves into a tuberculosis (TB) hospital. TB is a very contagious disease of the lungs, which causes coughing. He thought the dank, gloomy caves might cure TB patients. He built 11 cabins inside a cave for his patients. Two soon died, the rest got worse, and the doctor himself died from TB too. The slab of stone, upon which the bodies of the dead patients were laid before being removed from the cave, is called Corpse Rock, and some say you can still hear the haunting sounds of coughing there.

A Ghoulish Guide

A slave named Stephen Bishop who worked as a guide for visitors to the caves died of an unknown cause in 1857. He had been an expert on the Mammoth Cave System and one of its greatest explorers. Bishop discovered many of the cave's tunnels and passages, and the blind, ghostly white fish swimming in the underground Echo River. Some people believe Bishop's ghost still lingers here. Visitors claim to have seen him, although others say it could be just shadows cast by the lights in the caves.

Death in the Darkness

The underground tunnels and chambers of the Mammoth Cave System were also used as a burial ground by groups of ancient Native American people. Several **mummies** have been found in the dark depths of the caves. The remains of an ancient Native American woman found in the entrance of a chamber known as Short Cave were very well **preserved** within the cave environment. One ancient Native American man had likely been mining gypsum from inside the cave when he became trapped beneath a large boulder and died.

Are the vast tunnels and chambers of the Mammoth Cave System haunted by those who died there?

CHAPTER 5

SPOOKY STONES

Nature has carved some weird rock forms but others were created by people long ago. Sometimes, these spooky stones were used to perform rituals or to mark places where ancient people buried their dead. Many of them still send tingles down the spines of people who visit these curious creations today.

Spooky Stone Circles

There are thousands of stone circles around the world. A stone circle is a circle or oval of huge rocks that ancient people carefully arranged. No one is certain why they were built or what they were used for. Perhaps some marked places where people met and spent time together. It seems more likely that the circles were places for ceremonies and ancient worship.

The Stonehenge Giants

The stone circle at Stonehenge in the UK is made of giant stones that tower above the landscape. Each stone is the equivalent weight of around four African elephants! There are different ideas about how the stone circle was created... One legend claims that Stonehenge was formed when ancient giants were suddenly turned to stone while dancing in a circle!

SPOOKED!

At the stone circle in Avebury in the UK, people report seeing strange, ghostly figures dancing around the stones at night, or of hearing spooky singing when there is no one else around. Some people say standing within the circles makes them feel full of dread. Others say they can feel vibrations from within Earth when standing there.

A Wizarding Way with Stones?

Other legends suggest that Stonehenge was created with the help of Merlin, the legendary magician of King Arthur of Britain. The stone circle was said to come from Ireland, where it had been built by giants. The giants had stolen the stones from Africa because they had magical properties. England's king sent Merlin with an army to get the stones from Ireland. The English army won the battle against the Irish army but couldn't move the huge stones, so Merlin used his magical powers to move them to England.

Stones and Ceremonies

People have figured out that the circle of stones at Stonehenge was built to line up with the longest and shortest days in the year, when the Sun is highest or lowest in the sky at noon. This suggests that Stonehenge was a place where these special days were marked with important ceremonies.

We still don't know for certain how the stones arrived at Stonehenge, but it is likely that this ancient place was very special to people who lived long ago.

The Chachapoya people seem to have believed that the dead carried on living among them, so they wanted them to be seen.

Stone Warriors of the Cloud Forest

Look up into the misty forests high in the Andes Mountains in Peru and you will see some spooky faces staring eerily out into the distance! The Chachapoya people lived high in the Andes and were known as the Warriors of the Clouds. They buried their dead in tombs carved to look like people high up on ledges on the steep mountainside.

Watching Over the Land

The Chachapoya buried important people high up in difficult-to-reach places. The Chachapoya tombs are up to 8 feet (2.4 m) tall and made of mud, wood, and straw. Each has a colorfully painted, oversized head and looks out over the valley below. Inside, there were once mummies of the dead, and offerings, but these have been removed by **looters** and archeologists.

The Chachapoya people fought bravely but were finally conquered by the Inca people in the late fifteenth century. They seemed to have struck fear into Inca hearts, however, because the Inca are said to have believed that the souls of these cloud warriors continued to roam the region.

It is believed the Tiwanaku statues represent stone giants that lived in the Andes before people.

The Birth of the Stone People

In the Andes mountains on the border of Bolivia and Peru there is an ancient legend that says a god of creation arose from Lake Titicaca. He ordered the Sun, Moon, and stars to rise too. This god then traveled to nearby Tiwanaku, where he created men and women from stones. Later, the creator god became unhappy with the world and the people he had created. He caused a terrible storm that brought floods and darkness, which almost wiped out all of the people on Earth. People told stories of terrifying giant floods in this area about 12,000 years ago that would have swept ancient people away.

Stone Giants

Today, imposing stone giants still stand guard over the ancient town of Tiwanaku. There are dozens of massive humanlike sculptures there, all made of stone dug from nearby sacred mountains and carved of sandstone or volcanic stone. Some of the sculptures even seem to carry weapons. When the Inca found Tiwanaku 200 years after its people had left, they thought that the stone figures were the remains of giants the god of creation had made before creating the people of the Andes.

EASTER ISLAND

Stone Heads

Staring out from a remote island in the middle of the Pacific Ocean are some fearsome-looking stone faces. These giant stone heads appear all over the island and as you look up at them, they give you a spooky feeling—it seems as if they are watching you! The massive stone figures, known as moai, were often built on top of platforms along the coast. They faced inland, as if to keep watch over the local people.

Gods in Stone?

Moai means "so that he can exist" and each figure on the island represents an important leader or ancestor. Legends say that the moai represent chiefs who were believed to be **descended** from the gods. They had supernatural powers to protect the community. Some also wear a cylinder of red stone on their heads, which may represent a chief's headdress.

....
The moai have long sloping noses, strong eyebrows, and large chins.

Making the Moai

There are around 1,000 moai. They are up to 32 feet (10 m) tall and weigh up to 82 tons (74 mt) each—this is twice the weight of the stones at Stonehenge. It is hard to imagine how the enormous moai were made before people invented cranes and forklifts. Evidence suggests they were carved by stone chisels made from a very hard type of rock.

Magical Powers

Legend has it that hundreds of years ago, a chief on Rapa Nui island had such great magical powers that the giant statues obeyed when he ordered them to walk to the spots on the island where they would like to stand.

Archeologists Say...

Rather than believing in the magical powers of the chief, archeologists believe that islanders transported the maoi to their resting places on wooden sleds. Then, they were moved along on rollers made from giant logs to their destinations. The figures may also have been put on a wooden rocker and pulled from side to side, rocking them along to the places where they stand.

Secret Stones

The island of Rapa Nui is so **isolated** in the Pacific Ocean that the moai remained a secret for thousands of years. It wasn't until 1722, when Dutch explorers stepped off their ships onto the island, that anyone outside the island saw the strange figures. Because the explorers arrived on the island on Easter Sunday, they gave it the name "Easter Island."

CHAPTER 6

HIDDEN CITIES

Early on in human history, people hunted and gathered food and moved from place to place. Later, they started to settle into farming communities that eventually grew into cities. Many of these cities became large and powerful and some became the centers of mighty empires. But even the most important cities have fallen or disappeared in the mists of time.

Lost in Time

Some remarkably powerful cities have appeared and then disappeared. Sometimes, a city is suddenly lost, for example, if there is a flood, earthquake, or other natural disaster. Sometimes, the decline is more gradual. Perhaps the weather changes and people cannot grow enough food or they move to a better location. Whatever the reason, walking in a hidden or lost city, haunted by the memories of those who once lived there, is an eerie experience you'll never forget.

A Lost City?

For many years, there had been stories of a mysterious city, hidden for 1,000 years in the steamy, tangled jungles of Cambodia. Then, in 2012, scientists began to study the dense jungle from above, using a laser-scanning device called LiDAR strapped to a helicopter. This device could see through the thick layer of leaves and trees to find the ruins of a whole city buried below. This was part of the huge lost city of Mahendraparvata, or the Mountain of Indra, King of the Gods.

A City in Decline

Why did this magnificent city disappear beneath the dense leaves of the jungle? The city on the mountain top was carefully planned, but perhaps one part of its design led to its downfall. Its position on top of the mountain was not ideal for growing rice and other crops. The city seemed to have been left before it was completed. Perhaps the residents couldn't figure out how to get enough water for farming. The lack of water could be one reason the unfinished city was abandoned.

Aceredo Village in Spain was abandoned in 1992 when the lands and buildings in the surrounding area were flooded to create a reservoir. Thirty years later, the eerie remains of this flooded town reappeared following a lengthy dry spell, which made water levels in the reservoir drop.

The ghost village of Aceredo in Spain was hidden for years but reappeared in 2022 after a drought.

Buried Under the Ground

The strange underground city of Derinkuyu in Turkey remained hidden for hundreds of years. It was found only in 1963 by a local man. At one time, this eerie city could shelter as many as 20,000 people, along with animals and food stores. There were even chapels inside its cavelike rooms. People could have remained hidden underground here for months at a time.

Secrets of Derinkuyu

Derinkuyu was like an underground fortress. It was hidden around 280 feet (85 m) below the surface. The cavelike rooms inside Derinkuyu stretched for miles. There were 18 floors of tunnels and each floor could be closed off separately. Giant boulders acted as doors to block the entrances between each of the floors. These could only be moved or opened from the inside. Each of the heavy doors had a small, round hole in it, just large enough for the people inside to spear any invaders who dared to try to enter.

The people of Derinkuyu built their secret underground city to escape dangerous enemies.

Were these carefully created cliff dwellings abandoned because of a dark history of violence and even cannibalism?

Cliff Dwellers

In around CE 1250, the Anasazi people left their villages in open land to build homes high up in the cliffs. The Mesa Verde National Park in Colorado contains more than 600 cliff houses built mainly from sandstone, wood, and a muddy mortar. The Anasazi built these homes under overhanging cliffs to protect them from the weather and perhaps from enemies. Archeologists believe the Anasazi felled tree trunks and cut notches for steps using stone axes. The steps were used to make log ladders for people to get to the entrance to their cliff dwellings.

Abandoned Village

But suddenly, a generation later, the Anasazi abandoned their village and they moved again. What awful event forced the Anasazi to flee? One explanation is attack by enemy tribes. Or perhaps water or other resources in the area were becoming scarce.

SPOOKED!

Many archeologists believe there is a more sinister reason the Anasazi left their village. They think that the leaders tried to rule their people with greater violence, killing them and even eating those who disagreed with them. This feeling of fear spread until the villagers started attacking, killing, and then eating each other.

POMPEII

A Busy and Bustling City

Nearly 2,000 years ago, Pompeii was a lively, busy Roman city basking in the sunshine of southern Italy. Then, one terrible day, the nearby Mount Vesuvius volcano suddenly erupted. The blast sent ash, rock, and scorching-hot volcanic gases high up into the air. The sky became black as the ash blocked out the Sun.

On the Run

Some people ran away from the city. Others chose to take shelter in their homes. Then, the ash started to fall from the sky, clogging the air and making it difficult to breathe. The ash piled up on roofs and became so thick and heavy that buildings collapsed. The ash blocked doorways, trapping people inside their homes.

Buried in Ash

The following day, a deadly blast of superheated gas and broken rock raced down the side of the volcano toward the city of Pompeii. It destroyed everything and everyone in its path. It moved so quickly, there was no chance of escape. The city and the 2,000 unfortunate people still there were buried under millions of tons of choking, deadly volcanic ash.

A Ghost Town?

Then in 1748, a group of explorers discovered that beneath the thick layer of dust and debris, Pompeii was mostly intact. The powdery volcanic ash that had buried the city had helped to preserve it. It was as if the city had been frozen in time. Most of its buildings were still standing, and everyday objects and household goods were still scattered in the streets. Walking through them gave an eerie impression of walking through a ghost town.

Trapped in Time

The spookiest thing of all was that the bodies of men, women, children, and animals were all preserved just as they had fallen. Many of the bodies that archeologists uncovered were still holding valuable household objects they were hoping to escape with as they tried to leave the city. Some bodies were found with their arms around each other, hugging one another close in their last moments. Others show the victims' last facial expressions at the moment of death.

After Pompeii was buried under a thick carpet of volcanic ash, the city was abandoned and lost for almost 2,000 years.

GLOSSARY

alkaline a chemical that can dissolve in water

ancestors people who are related to someone and lived before them

archeologists people who study history through artifacts and remains

bacteria tiny living things

barren describes a place that is dry and empty with few or no plants

blood rituals ceremonies that involve the release of blood

descended related to someone who lived long ago

dissolved mixed with a liquid and became part of the liquid

downstream in the direction in which a stream or river flows

Dreamtime the time of creation in the mythology of Australian Aboriginal people

fossilized became preserved in rock

freshwater water that is not salty and undrinkable like seawater

gypsum a colorless, white, or yellowish mineral, which is a substance found naturally in rock

Ice Age the time when Earth was covered in ice, 2.6 million to 11,700 years ago

isolated being completely alone

jade a green precious stone

legend a traditional story

looters people who steal during a war or riot

microorganisms living things so tiny they can only be seen with a microscope

mummies dead bodies that have been preserved

nocturnal describes something that is active at night

Norse belonging or relating to Scandinavian countries

predators animals that hunt and eat other animals

preserved treated in a particular way to keep in the same condition

remains a person's body after death

sacrifices animals or people killed to honor a god or gods

Scandinavian belonging to a group of northern European countries that includes Denmark, Norway, Finland, and Sweden

shamans people believed to have powers to heal sick people or to remove evil spirits from them

sinister evil and threatening

suffocation death caused by a lack of air to breathe

underworld the mythical world of the dead, imagined as being under Earth

wilt to become limp and drooping

FIND OUT MORE

Books

Ganeri, Anita. *Amazing Earth: The Most Incredible Places from Around The World*. Dorling Kindersley, 2021.

The Spectacular Science of Planet Earth. Kingfisher, 2023.

Weird But True! 2023. National Geographic Kids, 2022.

Websites

Learn about more spooky landforms at:
www.amergeog.org/2017/10/29/10-strange-geographical-formations

Discover some amazing facts about Death Valley at:
www.doi.gov/blog/12-things-you-didnt-know-about-death-valley

There's more to find out about Pompeii at:
https://facts.net/pompeii-facts

Read about spooky cenotes at:
www.mexicolore.co.uk/maya/home/sacred-sinkholes

Publisher's note to educators and parents:
All the websites featured above have been carefully reviewed to ensure that they are suitable for students. However, many websites change often, and we cannot guarantee that a site's future contents will continue to meet our high standards of educational value. Please be advised that students should be closely monitored whenever they access the Internet.

INDEX

About the Author
Louise Spilsbury is an award-winning children's book author. She has written countless books about history and science. In writing and researching this book, she is more spooked than ever by the idea that there are very spooky places out there!